Justin's tearin' up my heart!

It's all here! Learn about your favorite 'N Sync guy, Justin Timberlake!

When did Justin first discover fame?
What does he do when he's not performing?
Who are his music idols?
Could YOU be the perfect girl for him?

Find all these answers and more in . . .

'N Sync with Justin!

'N SYNC
with
justin

Matt Netter

AN ARCHWAY PAPERBACK
Published by POCKET BOOKS
New York   London   Toronto   Sydney   Tokyo   Singapore

AN ARCHWAY PAPERBACK *Original*

An Archway Paperback published by
POCKET BOOKS, a division of Simon & Schuster Inc.
1230 Avenue of the Americas, New York, NY 10020

Copyright © 1999 by Matt Netter

ISBN: 0-671-03276-3

First Archway Paperback printing March 1999

10 9 8 7 6 5 4 3 2 1

AN ARCHWAY PAPERBACK and colophon are registered trademarks of Simon & Schuster Inc.

Cover photos courtesy of London Features International

Printed in the U.S.A.

IL 4+

To every girl whose nights are filled with dreams of their favorite pop star, happy Valentine's Day.

To my mom, Terry, heart-shaped boxes full of sweets "for the girl who has everything."

Special thanks to the sweethearts at Pocket Books—Lisa, Liz, and Jane.

contents

introduction

Moments before the stage lights go on, a ray of sunshine takes the stage and warms the heart of every fixated girl in the crowd. The hearts melt when bright star Justin Timberlake flashes his million-dollar smile. The sold-out audience of thousands has come to hear and see 'N Sync, the most popular group in the world, perform a concert. Many of them will forget all that and spend the next hour and a half following the white hot eighteen-year-old's every move on stage.

Justin eats up the adulation with a spoon. During a performance of 'N Sync's hit "Tearin' Up My Heart," he sings, "if you want me girl, let me know" and cups his hand to his ear to incite a response from the crowd. Later, while shaking his hips to the beat of the smash "I Want You Back," he sings, "you're the one I want, you're the one I need" and points right at a girl in the second row who nearly faints. As Justin points, he notices all the banners. Like ship sails hovering over the sea of fans, each one is a testimony of love to him— "Justin—You Rock My World," "Justin's Da Bomb," "Bounce Is All That," "Justin, Will You Be Mine?"

The concert concludes with the beautiful harmonies of "God Must Have Spent a Little More Time on You." Many in the crowd have their own ideas about who God must have spent a little more time on. Justin croons, "I never thought that love could feel like this, when you changed my world with just one kiss" and piercing shrieks fill the air, tears stream and girls swoon, all in homage to their dream guy. Justin takes a bow together with his four band mates, JC Chasez, Chris Kirkpatrick, Joey Fatone, and Lance Bass, who never show the slightest twinge of jealousy and instead just soak in the applause.

"He's our favorite too," Chris says of his blue-eyed, blond-haired band mate. "It's all good. He's just got that star quality. When people see Justin on stage, they think he's really cool," JC, Justin's co–lead singer, roommate, and longtime friend, adds. In a short while, 'N Sync has achieved a level of success beyond the young quintet's wildest dreams— platinum records, hit songs, TV specials, a world tour, and millions of adoring fans. "We do the music for our fans," Lance explained in the group's home video *'N the Mix*. "They make us who we are."

'N Sync fans have made Justin Randall Timberlake the most eligible teen star in the world. He's been called the next Nick Carter. Justin shrugs at the notion. "I don't pay attention to stuff like that," he said in a *Teen People* magazine cover story. What he does pay attention to is his music, his band mates, family, and his growing legion of avid fans.

So, what's it like for an eighteen-year-old to feel the constant heat of the spotlight? What is Justin really like? What kind of girl is this single guy looking for? What are his hobbies, interests, quirks, likes, and dislikes? What's life like on the road for him and his band mates? What does his future hold? And how did Justin go from a Tennessee tot, to a Mouseketeer, to a worldwide sensation? Find out everything you ever wanted to know about the guy who's been tearin' up your heart—Justin Timberlake.

'N SYNC
with
justin

1
a born performer

From Memphis, Tennessee, to Orlando, Florida, to New York, Los Angeles, and everywhere in between, to Europe, Asia, Australia, Africa, South and Central America, millions of people from all corners of the world, of different languages, cultures, and customs, know who Justin Timberlake is. To many adults he's just "the curly-haired guy from 'N Sync," but to kids and teens everywhere, he's a superhero.

Though superhero is a term usually reserved for the likes of Batman and Wonder Woman, it's as appropriate a classification you'll find for a guy who's far too talented to be human. What special powers does he possess? He has an angelic voice that can steal your ear, an adorably warm smile that can melt your heart, and an endearing charm that can make you love him. While he may not use his powers to save lives on a daily basis, he has his own superhero duties, like churning out hit records, selling out concert arenas, and bringing joy to millions of fans. Incredibly, the seemingly immortal Justin is not from another planet, but from Memphis, Tennessee. And, as impossible as it is to believe, he's just a regular teen with hopes and dreams just like you, only his wildest ones have come true.

God Must Have Spent a Little More Time on Him

"Man, I'm havin' the time of my life," Justin gloated on MTV. "There's people out there who dream of being actors and actresses and there's people out there who dream of being astronauts. The thing that's special about what I do, to me, is that I love to do it." Justin is on cloud nine because as a member of 'N Sync he is fulfilling his life's dream to entertain. From before he could walk it was obvious that Justin was a born performer. Years of practice, hard work, persistence, guidance, adversity, and even a little luck have put Justin on top of the world.

These days, you won't find a teen magazine in America that doesn't feature a story on 'N Sync and a gorgeous pinup of their youngest member staring back at you. Even magazines like *TV Hits* in Australia, *Smash Hits* in Great Britain and *Big!* in Europe are giving their young fans a healthy dose of the blond-haired, blue-eyed boy wonder. As one teen magazine editor told the author, "Justin's popularity with our readers has surpassed Leonardo DiCaprio, Taylor Hanson, and even Nick Carter. He's *it*." Justin's still just getting used to celebrity status. "I don't know what to say to that," he told *16* magazine.

In spite of his disbelief, Justin's rise to glory was more progressive than it was for his band mates. Having begun his career as an entertainer at an earlier age and with several years of talent shows, followed by a two-year stint on *The Mickey Mouse Club*, under his belt, Justin has gradually, if not methodically, eased his way into fame and fortune. Yet, in his eighteen years, Justin has risen from tireless toddler, to singing sensation, to TV teen, to lead singer of one of the most famous pop groups in the world. It all began eighteen years ago.

Memphis Munchkin

When Memphis, Tennessee natives Randy and Lynn Timberlake found out they were expecting their first child, they had no idea they were about to introduce the world to a new star. On January 31, 1981, a beautiful baby boy was born and they christened him Justin Randall Timberlake. "I think I was born at Saint Jude Medical Center or another children's medical center in Memphis, Tennessee," Justin tried to remember for *Super Teen* magazine.

Lynn and Randy brought their curly, blondcoifed, blue-eyed bundle of joy back to their home in Memphis, Tennessee, where they proudly introduced him to his family, friends, and neighbors. From that day, Justin's parents knew they had something special on their hands. By the time he was a toddler, Justin made it obvious that he liked being the center of attention. Lynn sang to him and played music for him, to which he was quite responsive, and by the time he could talk, Justin began singing.

"I've been singing since I was two," Justin told *Teen People* magazine. "If I could talk, I could sing. I was always performing for somebody." Indeed he was. Justin's relatives recall that at Christmas, Justin demanded every guest's attention by dancing around, singing, or telling jokes. As a tot, Justin even toted around a little plastic guitar. Dad, Randy, who was in a bluegrass band and has a beautiful voice himself, encouraged little Justin's singing.

Randy and Lynn divorced when Justin was

young, and both have since remarried. Lynn married Paul Harless, a Memphis banker, who now flies to Orlando to be with his family on weekends. Though Justin still maintains a relationship with his birth father, Randy, his wife, Lisa, and their two boys, Jonathan, five, and Steven, eight months, he was raised mostly by his mother and stepfather.

Though divorce is tough on any kid, Justin still had a very normal childhood filled with love and joy. Justin grew up part of a big family that included two sets of loving parents and four sets of doting grandparents, as well as plenty of pets, including two dogs, Scooter and Ozzie, and two cats, Millie and Alley. Whichever way he turned, Justin was showered with support, encouragement, and affection. In the *'N Sync* liner notes, Justin thanked "My parents for loving the whole world, and for showing me the way to do that, for loving me (even when it's hard!) and for being so supportive of me. My grandparents for giving me everything (I mean everything!) right down to their hearts. Thanks to all my other family members for supporting me."

The Whiz Kid

Justin attended elementary school in Memphis, but it was immediately clear that he was not like all the other kids. "I'm not gonna necessarily say I was a good kid in school," Justin admitted to *Tiger Beat* magazine, "but I was in good with all the teacher and principals, so I never got in trouble." Justin found one outlet for his considerable energies in basketball and another in singing.

As a kid, Justin idolized the world's most famous Michaels, Jackson and Jordan. After school, he would play basketball for hours on end, pretending to score the winning basket like his hero Michael Jordan. Whenever darkness or inclement weather didn't allow for basketball, Justin stayed indoors listening to Stevie Wonder on his parents' stereo and pretending to be Michael Jackson, dancing and singing around the house.

To this day, Justin swears, "my voice is my most prized possession." Mom, Lynn, recognized that, and when he was eight years old, she signed Justin up for singing lessons. He got additional vocal practice from singing in the choir, like his father, grandparents, and many other relatives before him. "I grew up singing in church," Justin told *Teen Beat* magazine. "Then I got into voice lessons when I was about eight. Then I did talent shows and things, and from that moment on, I knew that's what I wanted to do."

Among those talent shows was a stage performance at the Grand Ole Opry, a golden opportunity that Justin still treasures. When Justin was ten, he was part of a little group that emulated New Kids on the Block, the 'N Sync of the late '80s and early '90s. They sang New Kids songs at a school production and then began performing at other local schools, developing a small following along the way.

Justin's big break however, would come in 1992 when he was eleven years old. The long running TV talent showcase *Star Search* held a talent search in Memphis, and Justin was chosen to appear on the show. Justin and his mom flew to Orlando, Florida, where the show is taped. As a Junior Vocalist contestant, Justin had the once-in-a-lifetime opportunity to put his singing and dancing talents on display for both the studio audience and millions of television viewers.

Though his rendition of a country song didn't win him the competition, Justin was a winner nonetheless. As luck would have it, a Disney Channel casting director was in the crowd and was quite impressed with the looks and talent of the eleven-year-old sensation. The Disney executive approached Justin and his mom and told them about an open audition for new cast members of the Disney Channel's long-running franchise, *The Mickey Mouse Club.*

Justin and Lynn headed back to Memphis where the audition was to be held. Thirty thousand kids auditioned and shining star Jus-

tin was one of just seven selected to join the
cast for the 1993 season. With that, the excited mother and son packed their belongings
and flew down to Orlando to take up new
residence near Disney-MGM Studios where
MMC is filmed.

2
from memphis to MMC

Moving to Orlando meant saying good-bye to Memphis and leaving behind family, friends, school, and basketball. Early on, it wasn't easy for Justin to adapt to life in a new place, but Orlando provided sunshine, new friends, and countless opportunities. Between going to school, playing basketball, and being a part of *The Mickey Mouse Club,* Justin made new friends at every turn. In fact, in sixth grade, Justin had his first girlfriend, an *MMC* cast member named Mindy.

One of the first friends Justin made was a seventeen-year-old *MMC* cast mate from Maryland named JC Chasez. "JC was on the show for four years," Justin explained in *Superteen* magazine, "and I joined two years after that.

So, actually, together, we did the show for two years, over on Sound Stage One [at MGM Studios]."

JC took an immediate liking to Justin. "He's the All-American guy," JC told *Rolling Stone* magazine. The boys' companionship developed into much more as Justin and JC began sharing their dreams of landing recording contracts. "We all had daydreams about being entertainers," Justin said on the Disney Channel's *'N Sync In Concert* special.

The Mickey Mouse Club

Disney's long running franchise, *The Mickey Mouse Club*, has entertained several generations of viewers while providing big breaks for a few hundred aspiring entertainers, several of which have gone on to achieve successful careers in movies, television, and music. In the late 1950s the black-and-white variety show introduced America to a group of fresh-faced stars, including its most famous alumnus, Annette Funicello. In the 1970s, the show, then called *The New Mickey Mouse Club,* was in color and featured a new generation of stars, including *The Facts Of Life*'s Lisa Whelchel.

When Justin was a cast regular for the 1993 and 1994 seasons it was known as *MMC.* The after-school club showcased the talents of twenty cast members, all aged eleven to eighteen, as part of a variety show. The cast sang, danced, did comedy skits, introduced guest stars, and even tackled important issues affecting teens. "You get to dip your fingers into everything," Justin told *All-Stars* magazine. "You're not restricted to one thing at all. Doing the comedy was a lot of fun. You weren't restricted to one kind of music either."

Each season, thousands of hopefuls auditioned for the twenty spots on the variety show. "We spent a lot of energy and effort not to find just the most talented kids, but kids who'd be welcomed into the home every day," the Disney Channel's head of programming told *USA Today* back when Justin was on *MMC.* Although he was just twelve and thirteen when he was on the show, Justin realized fully how special this opportunity was. "By far, it's one of the best things I've ever done in my whole life. I couldn't have thought of a better thing to do," Justin said in *All-Stars* magazine.

While Justin was part of the show, he had several cast mates who would also later graduate to bigger and better things. TV star Keri Russell (*Felicity*) and her real-life boyfriend Tony Lucca, who was on the Aaron Spelling show *Malibu Shores* and is currently working on a solo music career, were both fellow Mouseketeers, as were Ryan Gosling (*Young Hercules*) and upcoming pop music stars Nikki DeLeach (Innosense), Christina Aguilera, Britney Spears, and of course, JC Chasez.

JC was an *MMC* star for four years, from 1991 to 1994, the last two of which were together with Justin. "I would say that it was the experience of a lifetime," JC explained on an America Online interview. "We got to do all spectrums of the business, not just singing and dancing, but acting too. It's something that will be with us for the rest of our lives."

"I definitely think it helped with our music

because we got to sing a lot on the show," Justin added. At thirteen, Justin felt it was time to go back to school to "be a kid for a second." But, as he explained to *Teen People* magazine, the classroom just wasn't for him. "I got so bored and really down about everything. I started to get a little rebellious. I didn't really get into trouble, but I wasn't focusing like I could. I didn't have the inspiration that music gave me, and it hit me: That's my place in the world. That's where I belong."

3
in sync with JC

Justin headed to Nashville, Tennessee, where he met up with his old *MMC* pal JC, and the two young performers hooked up with a vocal coach. The coach separately worked with the two guys in the studio, where they each began working on solo projects. After discussing their plans for the future, Justin and JC realized they had similar ideas, and after harmonizing together, they discovered that they had similar singing styles and could perform together.

Another thing they had in common was that they were both very passionate about music and quite serious about pursuing a career in entertainment. "I'm a perfectionist. I want to give 150 percent every time," Justin told *BB* magazine. JC's sentiments exactly.

Two Plus Three Equals Five

Meanwhile, back in Orlando, two young singer/dancers with similar aspirations were hatching their own plans. Brooklyn-born Joey Fatone, a friend of JC's, and Pittsburgh native Chris Kirkpatrick, whom JC had befriended through Joey, were working as theme park performers at Universal Studios Florida when Chris, who'd been moonlighting as a coffee shop singer, came up with the idea to form a vocal group. After talking it over with Joey, he picked up the phone.

"Chris calls me and says, 'I want to get a group together,' and I immediately call JC," Justin recalled in the *'N the Mix* video. "JC knew Chris from Universal and I knew Chris from some auditions. I did some research through my old vocal coach and we found Lance." Lance, of course, is Mississippi born Lance Bass, the bass backup singer with the unmistakable sea green eyes.

"We really put ourselves together," Justin recalled in *Billboard* magazine. "It's funny to look back on how well we all came together; it just happened step by step." Justin and JC moved back to Orlando and, together with Chris, they moved in with Justin's mom, Lynn, in their home just steps from the warehouse where the band would begin rehearsing. Joey and Lance took up residence nearby. Justin would continue his education through independent study.

For several months, the guys would meet up at the warehouse at night and on weekends when they weren't working, or in Justin's case, going to school. Don't forget, he was only fourteen at this point. Luckily for Justin, his parents were very supportive of his new endeavor and encouraged him to go for it, while reminding him that if it became too difficult for him, he could quit anytime he wanted to.

There would be no need for that though as the video demo the guys put together themselves got them hooked up with Trans Continental Entertainment President Lou Pearlman and manager Johnny Wright, the same team that had launched the Backstreet Boys a few years earlier. Pearlman and Wright were impressed with the guys, not just for their talents, but for their solidarity too.

In a *Teen People* magazine feature, Justin offered up the following metaphor to illustrate the strength of the bond between the 'N Sync guys. "You take this finger and try to break it, and you'll be very successful. But, you take this fist—all five of these fingers together—and you won't. I guarantee that."

This incredibly strong union is a key part of 'N Sync's success. They got along like brothers from the beginning, and though they had their differences, they knew how to be diplomatic. "As far as making decisions, it's a democracy," Justin explained to *Tiger Beat* magazine. "It's good because we have an odd amount of people so it divides things up three to two."

One of the first decisions they would have to make as a band was to come up with a name. The ideal name would interlock all their names and represent their unity. "Actually, my mom came up with the name," Justin told *Teen Beat* magazine. "We shot it around and thought it was a good name to represent us. Shortly after we copyrighted it, we recognized that all the last letters of our names spelled 'N Sync." At least it does when you incorporate Lance's nickname, Lansten.

Big Time

With guidance from their new management, the guys polished their act and put together a solid demo. While Pearlman and Wright shopped the demo to record companies, Justin, JC, Lance, Chris, and Joey worked with a battery of vocal coaches, choreographers, and stylists to put the finishing touches on their act. They also learned invaluable lessons from their management about the record industry and the business side of music. "We learned a lot from Lou. He's taught us a little about the business," Justin remarked on MTV. In no time flat, 'N Sync landed a recording contract with BMG/RCA. It was the summer of 1996.

With less than a week to celebrate their good fortune, the quintet was flown to Europe, where they would spend more than a year. For a few months, the guys bounced back and forth between Sweden and Germany to record their album. Together with a talented group of producers, songwriters, and technicians, including Max Martin, Kristian Lundin, Veit Renn, Gary Carolla, Full Force, and the late Denniz PoP, 'N Sync created a brilliant debut album full of harmony-driven ballads and infectious dance pop tracks.

For the rest of 1997 'N Sync toured Europe, Asia, South Africa, and Mexico, performing concerts and promoting their wonderful debut CD. By the end of the year, half the world was hooked on the sounds of an exciting new band and in love with their endearing personalities and swoon-worthy good looks. Soon, everywhere they went, a crowd of admirers followed. "We usually have to take two or three bodyguards with us there," Justin said in *Billboard* magazine.

When the exhausting year came to a close,

the guys headed back to the U.S. and Orlando to rest up for a while, enjoy the holidays, and soak in their newfound success. "We certainly didn't expect things to go as well as they did in Europe," Justin told *Billboard* magazine. "We hope to have half as much success in the U.S."

4
'ncredible!

Upon introducing themselves to American music fans, comparisons to other pop groups, particularly the Backstreet Boys, were inevitable. "When we put our group together—and we were together for about six months before we met Johnny—I didn't even know who the Backstreet Boys were," Justin said in *Teen People* magazine.

"As far as image, we're just five guys doing the music that we like to do," Justin explained in *Billboard* magazine. "We don't pay attention to this boy band phenomenon. We just enjoy what we do and being on top and having fun. We consider ourselves a vocal group, because that's what we started off to do. We just want to entertain."

A Stateside Sensation

And entertain they did. In early 1998, 'N Sync made their American presence known by spending three months granting interviews and photo shoots to magazines and doing radio publicity, while RCA, their U.S. record company, worked overtime to get their first single, "I Want You Back," on the radio and the video on MTV. "The reason we're excited to release the single here in the U.S. is it's a little bit different from what you usually hear in pop," JC told *16* magazine. "A lot of things that have been released that weren't rocked out were ballads."

The American market, especially teens and kids, was incredibly receptive to both the 'N Sync single and video, sending "I Want You Back" to gold status and near the top of the pop charts. Once everybody was familiar with the song and the group, it was time to promote their debut album *'N Sync*, which was released in June of 1998. Justin, JC, Lance, Chris, and Joey spent the next three months flying all over the country doing record store promotions and radio publicity. They performed miniconcerts at malls and outside radio stations and record stores.

Then, in May, their big break came. The Disney Channel had pegged the Backstreet Boys to be a part of a televised *In Concert* special that would feature a live performance, theme park tour, and group interviews, but they were unavailable. Enter 'N Sync. Justin and his band mates brought their families along for the weekend-long taping of the special and had a blast. Little did they know that this weekend of fun would produce one of the highest-rated cable programs of the year, one that would air several more times over the summer.

Along with the release of their second single, "Tearin' Up My Heart," the Disney Channel special drove the sales of *'N Sync* to platinum status. Following the special, 'N Sync was suddenly in demand, and made dozens of TV appearances on talk shows and MTV, as well as charity events and major promotions like the Twix Twin Towers contest and the Virgin Megastore opening that caused a traffic jam in New York City! By the end of summer, 'N Sync's debut album had reached multiplatinum status and had soared to number two on the *Billboard* 200 album chart, surpassing the Backstreet Boys.

The overnight success left Justin speechless. "That was a little overwhelming," Justin recalled *Billboard* magazine. "When I found out the album had gone to number two, I was jumping up and down. I didn't know what to say."

Here to Stay

If 'N Sync came in like a lion, they closed out the year as kings of the jungle. While magazines like *Rolling Stone*, *Billboard*, and *Teen People* were doing features on 'N Sync, the band was preparing for their first major U.S. concert tour. They spent the month of October opening up for Janet Jackson on her highly successful Velvet Rope tour. This was yet another dream come true for Justin, who has her poster hanging in his bedroom and openly admits to having a crush on her. He likes her music too.

In the midst of the tour, 'N Sync found the time to put together quite a Christmas present to their fans: a holiday album, home video, and three TV Christmas specials, including another one for the Disney Channel. They also made a special appearance on *Sabrina, the Teenage Witch* and hosted several segments for MTV. *Home for Christmas* went platinum and *'N the Mix* topped the video charts as both made very popular stocking stuffers. Meanwhile, their third single, "God Must Have Spent a Little More Time on You," began making its own climb up the charts.

By the end of their first year in America, more than just the fans were recognizing 'N Sync. They took home two awards (Best New Artist Clip and Best Dance Clip for "I Want You Back") at the *Billboard* Music Video Awards and one more (Best New Artist) at the American Music Awards. They also performed the televised at *Billboard* New Year's Eve party.

Beginning in November, 'N Sync planned on going on their own eighteen-date headlining concert tour. After every concert sold out and the album skyrocketed to five times platinum, 'N Sync decided to extend the tour to all the way through May, giving many more of their fans a chance to see them perform. "We're pretty much booked until the spring [of 1999]," Justin told *16* magazine. Word was getting out that these guys knew how to put on a show.

'N Sync Live

"Tour life is busy, busy, busy, busy, busy. That's the main word for a tour," Justin said in the *'N the Mix* video. From flights, airports, limos, and hotels, to sound check, concerts, interviews, and photos, there isn't much time for rest on an 'N Sync tour. Somehow, they always manage to find time for meet-and-greets. Either before or after every single performance, the 'N Sync guys always set aside some time to sign autographs and pose for pictures with fans.

The concerts themselves are quite an experience, as any 'N Sync fan can attest. "Being original, that's another thing," Justin said in the *'N the Mix* video. "You just want to come out and do something different instead of something everybody's done." Such as kicking off a concert by coming out in space suits, encouraging audience sing-alongs and doing choreographed acrobatics onstage. Hours of rehearsals, both with their backup band and with their team of talented choreographers, as well as with the technical crew, have resulted in a phenomenal live show that has fans clamoring for more.

"Our live show is crazy," Justin explained on the *'N the Mix* video. "It's nonstop energy. The show just keeps rolling. We don't want our fans to have a moment in the show where their attention is not on us. We want all your attention when you come to the show."

Juggling Fame and Adversity

The maturity that Justin's demonstrated in handling fame has often made those around him forget that he is just a teenager. Justin thinks of his band mates as his best friends, calls his mom every day no matter where he is, and never forgets for a second how fortunate he is and how fleeting fame can be. The sudden influx of money and fame hasn't gone to Justin's head. Though he may drive a Mercedes, that's just a reward for his hard work. He's saving most of his money for the future and besides, money is not what it's about for Justin. He's made the sacrifices he has for his love of music and for his fans.

Being famous has its ups and downs as Justin has discovered. "We're very pleased with the progress we've made. We're nothing but happy and we love our fans," he told *16* magazine. "To know that you've touched them enough that they listen to your songs so often that they know them by heart—that's special," he added in *Bop* magazine.

Justin expanded on this point in 'N Sync's home video *'N the Mix*. "It always means something to me, the gratification I get from singing a song live and actually seeing the fans go crazy and then, all of a sudden, you could just stop singing the leads and put the mic in the audience and everybody sings the song. It's just the greatest feeling that fans pay that much attention and that they respect your music that much," he said.

Having millions of fans isn't all good though. Justin can't just go to the movies or to the mall whenever and wherever he wants too. In fact, every time he steps out the door, he runs the risk of being chased after by a throng of screaming fans. Sure, they mean no harm, but don't you think it would be nice to have a moment of privacy every now and then? "It's very hard to find your own peace and quiet," Justin revealed in an America Online interview. "You usually only find it in your hotel room because that's where you can go to sleep from your exhaustion."

What Justin likes best about being in 'N

Sync is "being able to make music, meet people, and travel." One of the best perks about being an entertainer is that you get to visit exotic places that most people never get to see. Justin and his band mates had the experience of a lifetime when they went to Capetown, South Africa, for a record company convention. Luckily, the guys had a break in the action while they were there that they took full advantage of by touring the rolling green hills and posing for pictures with a gorgeous cheetah.

As Justin has pointed out, however, traveling the world has its downside too. "We all get homesick, but we don't really talk about it. Anyway, the five of us are like a family and we all look out for each other," he explained in *Superteen* magazine. The biggest adjustment for Justin has been the time away from his home and family. "I kind of took that stuff for granted, seeing my family all the time. Now, I never get to see them anymore, and I always wonder what they're doing and things like that," he lamented.

Whatever the sacrifice, be it lack of sleep, privacy, or time with family, Justin feels it's a trade-off he'd make again without a moment's hesitation. "It's not that we mind. We love being in 'N Sync and we're having the time of our lives," Justin told *Teen Beat* magazine. "We love doing what we do. Maybe we don't get as much free time as we please, but that just comes with the territory."

Words to Live By

In Justin's bio from *MMC* he said that his philosophy on life was to "always strive to do your best and never give up," a credo he has certainly followed through on. In the *'N the Mix* video, Justin gave some helpful words of advice to young aspiring entertainers. "Whatever your dream is, you have to practice your craft and make it the best it can be."

5
supersongs
(& vivid videos)

To date, 'N Sync has two CDs (technically three, if you consider the U.S. and European versions of their debut), thirty-three songs, eight videos, and one home video. But with millions of fans who can't seem to quench their thirst for the sights and sounds of 'N Sync, you can look forward to many new songs and videos from the fab five in the future. Here's a rundown of the 'N Sync library, as it stood when this book was being written.

'N Sync

'N Sync's self-titled debut CD has spent over a full year on the *Billboard* 200 album chart. The now diamond album (five times platinum—five million copies sold in the U.S.) has reached as high as number two on the album chart. The slightly different European version of the CD achieved similar success overseas, going gold or platinum in over a dozen countries.

Of the thirteen tracks on *'N Sync,* "God Must Have Spent a Little More Time on You" is the one Justin likes best. "It's a slammin' song and it's my favorite one on our album," he said in 'N Sync's home video *'N the Mix.* "It relates to me a lot just because I'm a very spiritual person." Justin also has a sweet spot for the ballad because he finds the title and chorus to be romantic. "It's perfect the way it comes out. I think it's a wittier way of saying to someone how special they are."

Home for Christmas

As if all the radio play, fan mail, and accolades weren't enough indication that 'N Sync had arrived, they were asked by RCA records to quickly put together a holiday album in time for Christmas of 1998. Only established stars are given the opportunity to make Christmas albums. In the past decade such efforts have eluded countless pop groups and have been reserved for the likes of Celine Dion, Boyz II Men, and Mariah Carey. When *Home for Christmas* debuted at number six on the *Billboard* 200 album chart, 'N Sync had clearly sent the message that they were one of the biggest pop groups in the world and they were here to stay.

Home for Christmas includes fourteen tracks, eleven of them original 'N Sync recordings. Several of the same producers and songwriters who worked with the guys on *'N Sync*, including Veit Renn and Gary Carolla, as well as some new names, lent a hand in the recording process. Justin and JC cowrote the single "Merry Christmas, Happy Holidays" with Renn. This was Justin's second songwriting effort, having cowritten "Giddy Up" with his band mates and Renn, for their debut CD.

Dasher, Dancer, Donner, & Timberlake?

Making a holiday album was special to Justin for another reason. Christmas is his favorite holiday. "I'm a very spiritual person and that's the reason I love Christmas," Justin told *Tiger Beat* magazine. "Other than that, being with my family—Christmas time is always the best vacation time I have with my family. That's always been one of the most fun things for me."

Christmas was always a joyous occasion in Justin's home. He fondly remembers going skiing, trimming trees, eating hearty meals, and exchanging gifts with his family. "I remember when I got my first TV. That was great," he told *Superteen* magazine. "I had a Nintendo with it, so I was Super Mario-ed out. That was when I was very young. None of my friends had it yet, so I was like, 'Yeah, I'm so cool!'" Of course, being the sweetheart that he is, Justin follows the old adage It is better to give than to receive. "My mom didn't have any nativity scenes. She used to make ceramics and stuff, but I guess they had gotten lost," he explained. "So, I got her a stained-glass window with a nativity scene. When you put it in front of the light it's a beautiful thing."

Justin recalls singing Christmas carols with his mom as a kid too, making *Home for Christmas* that much more special for him. For the record, Justin's favorite Christmas song is "O Holy Night," which 'N Sync does a beautiful a cappella rendition of on *Home for Christmas.*

Let's Go to the Videotape!

'N Sync's music videos are unique in that they do more than just complement the feel and theme of the song. They give the viewer a strong sense of who the band members are individually. Part of this is a result of the input the guys have in the making of their videos. A second video was made for "I Want You Back" for America because the guys had changed so much and looked so different. The American version, however, went through some changes.

It originally featured backup dancers but that was cut and the one-on-one basketball game between Justin and Chris was added in.

"We could have done like a long story line, a totally make-believe thing," Justin explained in the *'N The Mix* home video, "but we figured, what better way than to just show off our skill and just do it." The guys couldn't have been more right, as the "I Want You Back" video went on to win two *Billboard* Music Video Awards. Justin and his band mates demonstrate their basketball skills again in the "Here We Go" video, which centers around all five guys playing a competitive five-on-five game in a gymnasium.

While 'N Sync's tour schedule can be grueling, their video shoot schedule is often more exhausting. Eighteen-hour days are not at all uncommon. In fact, the "Tearin' Up My Heart" video was filming for twenty-four hours straight. Though a fairly simple video that features the guys at a mock photo shoot and then dancing and hanging around in a warehouse, it has become a fan favorite because of one particular scene. Seeing Justin on a bed singing to the camera is almost too much to handle.

Catching glimpse of Justin under a waterfall on a deserted island is quite a sight to behold as well. The "For the Girl Who Has Everything" video delivers this visual treat. Filmed in Hawaii, the video had the guys forgetting they were working and not on vacation. Justin and his band mates got to goof off on the beach and go horseback riding during filming. The location was important to the theme of the video, in which the guys are shipwrecked on an island and discover a trunk full of items from "the girl who has everything." The romantic guys send the spoiled but forlorn girl a message in a bottle that includes their picture.

"For the Girl Who Has Everything" is one of the deeper 'N Sync songs and thus needed a story line video, as Justin explained in the 'N the Mix home video. "It's a good song. It's got a good R&B feel to it. It shows you that we're not just totally dance pop. We *can* actually sing. It's something a little bit more intricate, should I say." Justin's favorite song, "God Must Have Spent a Little More Time on You," is equally intricate (good word, Justin) and thus, also called for a story line video.

Dressed all in white, the 'N Sync guys seem to hover like angels in color above the alternating black-and-white story. The touching story is about the relationship between a mother and son and how, no matter how much he grows up and changes, he's always special in her eyes. When he goes off to fight in the war, he meets another girl and his mother worries that he's not coming home. At the end of the video, the son shows up at his mom's doorstep and she embraces him as if he were sent by angels.

The festive and fun video for "Merry Christmas, Happy Holidays" features fake snow, an imaginary sleigh ride, and a cameo by *Diff'rent Strokes* star Gary Coleman. The guys play the part of angels from above again as they bring food to the homeless and presents to needy children. Of course, they still find time to dance around the tree with some young girls too!

One 'N Sync video that you may not get to see is for the European single "U Drive Me Crazy." Filmed in Malibu, California, as a thank you for their German fans, who were the first to go 'nsane, the video is their funniest one yet. At a mock audition, the guys don wacky outfits and perform in front of judges to try and land a recording contract. The guys dress up as the Jackson 5, a heavy metal group, and even the Spice Girls before finally just being themselves and, of course, landing a record deal. Can you guess who was which Spice Girl? Chris was Scary (no surprise), Lance was Baby, JC was Posh, Joey was the lost Ginger, and Justin was Sporty.

'N the Mix

'N Sync's first home video, *'N the Mix*, is a must have for any fan. It features a behind-the-scenes look at their videos and includes concert clips, interviews, on the road and in home footage, and even childhood pictures of JC and Justin at the end. The seventy-five-minute video, which comes with a free poster, was a very popular Christmas present in 1998, selling over a million copies.

Discography

'N Sync

"Tearin' Up My Heart"
"I Just Wanna Be with You"
"Here We Go"
"For the Girl Who Has Everything"
"God Must Have Spent a Little More Time on You"
"You Got It"
"I Need Love"
"I Want You Back"
"Everything I Own"
"I Drive Myself Crazy"
"Crazy for You"
"Sailing"
"Giddy Up"

additional tracks on the European version of *'N Sync*
"Riddle"

"Best of My Life"
"More Than a Feeling"
"Together Again"
"Forever Young"

Singles

"I Want You Back"
"Tearin' Up My Heart"
"God Must Have Spent a Little More Time on
     You"
"For the Girl Who Has Everything"
"U Drive Me Crazy" [Europe only]
"Merry Christmas, Happy Holidays"

Home for Christmas

"Home for Christmas"*
"Under My Tree"*
"I Never Knew the Meaning of Christmas"*
"Merry Christmas, Happy Holidays"*
"The Christmas Song (Chestnuts Roasting On
     An Open Fire)"
"I Guess It's Christmas Time"*
"All I Want Is You This Christmas"*

"The First Noel"
"In Love on Christmas"*
"It's Christmas"*
"O Holy Night (A Cappella)"
"Love's In Our Hearts on Christmas Day"*
"The Only Gift"*
"Kiss Me at Midnight"*

*original 'N Sync track

Videography

"I Want You Back" [European version]
"I Want You Back" [U.S. version]
"Tearin' Up My Heart"
"God Must Have Spent a Little More Time on
      You"
"U Drive Me Crazy" [Europe only]
"Merry Christmas, Happy Holidays"
"Here We Go"
"For the Girl Who Has Everything"

N Sync: 'N the Mix—The Official Home Video

6
band mates & buds

Justin often refers to JC, Chris, Lance, and Joey as his "second family." When he's away from his home and family for long stretches at a time, Justin often leans on his band mates for support. "I have four friends that I'm doing this with, so if I ever get out of line about anything, they wouldn't hesitate to tell me," Justin told *Teen Machine* magazine. "It's just like that. We have a friendship that will never, ever, ever end. Even if we weren't 'N Sync, we would still be friends." It takes a very special group of guys to be band mates, friends, and family to each other. Justin's lucky enough to have found himself such a group.

JC

Justin has known twenty-two-year-old JC the longest from their days on *MMC* together. They've been friends for seven years now, and have worked together, played together, traveled together, and lived together. They are the lead singers of 'N Sync and the chemistry they demonstrate onstage, bouncing lyrics off one another while jumping and dancing in tandem, can be credited to their long-standing friendship. When performers are so in sync (pardon the pun) they are said to be "on the same page." Justin and JC are on the same line.

JC and Justin are virtually inseparable friends and they have a mutual respect for one another as people and performers. "I love his sincerity. He's a really nice genuine kind of person," JC told *TV Hits* magazine about his pal. Since they're as close as brothers, you can expect some level of competition between them. When time allows, the two guys love to play Nintendo, tease each other and, of course, play basketball. "Justin is very, very athletic. He's just always dying to do things and have a good time," JC added.

Full Name: Joshua Scott Chasez
Nickname: JC
Birth Date: August 8, 1976
Zodiac Sign: Leo
Birth Place: Washington, DC
Height: Five feet, ten inches
Weight: 150 pounds
Eye Color: Blue
Hair Color: Brown
Current Residence: Orlando, Florida
Parents: Karen and Roy
Siblings: 1 younger brother, Tyler (sixteen), and 1 younger sister, Heather (twenty)
Pets: Cat, Grendal

Chris

The wild and crazy guy of 'N Sync seems to be in a competition with A. J. McLean from

Backstreet Boys to see who can outdo the other guy with piercings, tattoos, hairdos, sunglasses, facial hair, and bandannas. It's a battle to the finish. May the best man win— don't worry, they're actually friends. They even have a crush on the same girl—No Doubt's Gwen Stefani. "He wanted to start that one. He totally sweats everything I do," Chris told *Teen Beat* magazine. "Funny how I did this way before he did. Get your own style man! Even if you're in a group with five guys, you can have your own personality. Be yourself!"

Chris isn't completely crazy, he'll just go to great lengths to have a good time, even if it's at his own expense. When he's not spinning records or doing something creative like drawing or writing music, Chris often spends his free time impersonating *South Park* characters, telling senseless jokes, making witty remarks, or prank calling friends. You may think Chris is silly, but when the 'N Sync guys are tired and homesick, guess who makes them laugh away the tears with a well-timed joke?

Full Name: Christopher Alan Kirkpatrick
Nicknames: Chris, Lucky
Birth Date: October 17, 1971
Zodiac Sign: Libra
Birth Place: Clarion, Pennsylvania
Height: Five feet, nine inches
Weight: 155 pounds
Eye Color: Brown
Hair Color: Brown
Current Residence: Orlando, Florida
Parents: Mom, Bev
Siblings: Four younger half sisters, Molly, Kate, Emily, and Taylor
Pets: None

Joey

"Joey's a very optimistic person," Justin told *TV Hits* magazine. "Whenever things aren't too good, he'll really try his hardest to make them better." Joey will usually do so by making people laugh, either intentionally or not. For one thing, he stands out from the other 'N Syncers like a sore thumb. His thick New York accent, on again/off again goatee, and vast collection of Superman hats, necklaces, and T-shirts easily make him one of the world's most easily recognizable pop stars. If, even with that description, you can't spot Joey in a crowded room, look for the guy talking with all the girls. "He's always chatting to girls. He's really flirtatious," Justin added. Justin gets a big kick out of Joey's wardrobe too, which includes bright colors, faux fur, and giant pants. "He wears some wacky stuff. Some of the outfits he goes out in are even wild for a club," Justin told *Teen Beat* magazine.

Full Name: Joseph Anthony Fatone, Jr.
Nicknames: Joey, Phat 1, Superman
Birth Date: January 28, 1977
Zodiac Sign: Aquarius
Height: Six feet
Weight: 175 pounds
Eye Color: Brown
Hair Color: Brown
Birth Place: Brooklyn, New York
Current Residence: Orlando, Florida
Parents: Phyllis and Joe

Siblings: One older brother, Steven, and one older sister, Janine

Lance

The more reserved quiet guy in 'N Sync, the one with sea green eyes and bass voice, is the aptly named Lance Bass. Or, as his band mates sometimes refer to him, Scoop. "The guys call me Scoop cuz whenever they ask me about our itinerary, I always know, " Lance explained in *Live & Kicking* magazine. Responsible and business-minded Lance had begun taking courses at the University of Nebraska but had to put his college plans on hold for 'N Sync. The dynamic guy even had aspirations of joining the space program at NASA.

Just because Lance is a bit shy and laid back, doesn't mean he doesn't know how to have a good time. The Mississippi crooner loves going to the beach and going jet skiing, as he demonstrates in the "I Want You Back" video. Lance also considers himself a movie buff, loves being outdoors, and collects Beanie Babies.

Full Name: James Lance Bass
Nicknames: Lansten, Scoop
Birth Date: May 4, 1979
Zodiac Sign: Taurus
Birth Place: Clinton, Mississippi
Height: Five feet, ten inches
Weight: 155 pounds
Eye Color: Green
Hair Color: Blond
Current Residence: Orlando, Florida
Parents: Diane and Jim
Siblings: One older sister, Stacy
Pets: None

7

bouncin' around

Basketball. Since you can't say ten words about Justin without mentioning it, let's get it out of the way. That said, Justin is in many ways just a normal teenage boy. Despite his good looks, fame, and talents, he puts his pants on one leg at a time just like you do. He has likes and dislikes, things that interest him, and things that bore him. There are many aspects to his personality and he has moods, emotions, and opinions just like you do. Onstage Justin is a superstar. Backstage he's just a guy.

The Boy Who Has Everything

TV Hits magazine asked Justin to describe himself in one sentence. "I'm an athletic, nice sorta guy," he responded. Away from the spotlight and the screaming fans, Justin's optimism, which stems from loving life and loving what he does, seems to rub off on everyone around him. Justin is a charming, upbeat, and likable guy who seems to get along well with everyone. He also enjoys some quiet time alone from time to time, only some people have mistaken this for something else. "People think that since I'm into myself a lot, that I am stuck up," he admitted on the group's website.

Another misconception about Justin is that he's arrogant. Despite his good looks and confidence, he's eaten his humble pie. He doesn't take himself too seriously, never bosses anyone around, and isn't the least bit vain. He says compliments make him blush. In fact, about the only time Justin catches himself looking in the mirror is when he's struggling with his hair. When it gets too long, it curls, but Justin's learned how to control it . "I grew my hair out once and I'd wake up every morning and look just like Maxwell. Boom!

Whoa! My hair was scaring me," he told *Tiger Beat* magazine.

There are many, many good things to say about Justin. He's a good son, a cool older brother, a loyal friend, an awesome band mate, and let's not forget, a hottie. Is Justin perfect? No. He says his biggest faults are lacking patience and procrastinating. He also wishes he was taller and had straighter hair. He burps a lot, is afraid of snakes, talks in his sleep, and won't even speak to anyone in the morning until he's had his bowl of cereal. Don't worry though, his Matt Damonesque smile will make you forget all about his shortcomings.

Regular Joe

Given a rare free day to do whatever he chooses, Justin says he'd "sleep, go to the gym if I've got the energy." Not so glamorous, is it? When the jet set lifestyle slows down for a moment, Justin, and his band mates alike, savor the chance to catch their breath. Justin spends his free time much the way you do, watching television and videos, playing Nintendo, and listening to music. "I go to parties, hang out with my friends. I like to do everything that someone my age likes to do," he explained in the 'N *the Mix* video.

While he's out for a drive in his candy-apple red M-class Mercedes, he might look for a pickup basketball game at the playground, go to the gym, or even hit the mall. "I'm a bit of a shopaholic," Justin told *TV Hits* magazine. His most likely purchases are CDs, clothes, candles, or gifts for his family. Justin goes to the gym to stay fit, but also because "working out always puts me in a calmer state of mind," he told *Superteen* magazine.

When the sun goes down, Justin's social options are somewhat limited. At eighteen, he remains too young to get into some of the dance clubs that the over-twenty-one Chris, Joey, and JC like to hang out at. "I'm a real party animal, when the others let me go to parties," he admitted to *Tiger Beat* magazine. While those three are all out movin', groovin', hoppin', and poppin' at a trendy night spot,

Justin is likely spending time at home with his parents or out with his fellow under-twenty-one band mate, Lance.

My Two Families

Justin savors every chance he gets to spend time with his family—*both* families. When 'N Sync gets their Christmas break, Justin spends his holiday with his mom, Lynn, and stepfather Paul, as well as grandparents and other family in the Orlando area. Justin's Orlando home is also where his dog, Ozzie, and cat, Alley, live, not to mention band mates JC and Chris.

Now that her boy, Justin, is all grown up and on his own, mom Lisa has forged a new career for herself as a music manager. Her self-made company, JustinTime Management, is aptly named after the apple of her eye. The main act she is representing is the upcoming all-girl group Innosense, who, like 'N Sync, were launched by Orlando-based Trans Continental Entertainment. The similarities don't end there, either. Like Justin and JC, one of the girls in the group, Nikki DeLoach, also

(Dennis Van Tine/London Features)

Justin Timberlake

(Jeffrey Mayer/Star File)

God Must Have Spent a Little More Time on *Them!*

(Miranda Shen/Celebrity Photo)

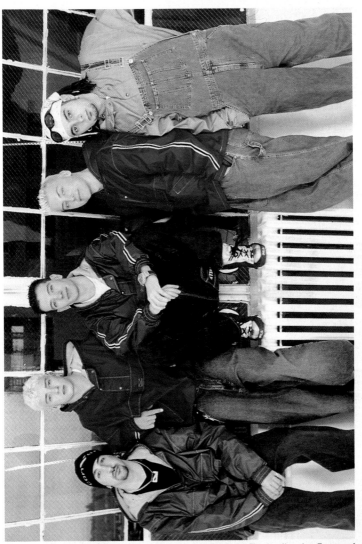

(Anthony Cutajar/London Features)

'N Sync

(Anthony Cutajar/London Features)

Curly

got her big break with *MMC*. Justin has taken an interest in his mom's new career and often discusses the ins and outs of the music business with her.

When Justin finds other free time, he heads back to Tennessee, where his father, Randy, stepmom, Lisa, and younger half brothers, Jonathan and Steven, live. Justin loves spending time with his little brothers. "In the last couple of years I haven't gotten to see my family too much, and I've become a real family-oriented person," Justin revealed in *Superteen* magazine. "Me personally, I've just become closer emotionally to my family."

Bounce Me the Ball

In the *'N the Mix* video, Justin explained with a shrug and a smile, "I play basketball. That's what I do, man. I'm not old enough to go clubbin'." He's been dribbling, shooting, and passing since he could walk, hence the nickname Bounce. All throughout school, singing lessons and talent shows, and even his two-year stint on *MMC*, Justin continued playing his favorite sport. As a kid he idolized Michael Jordan. When his homework was done, he ran outside to his driveway or to the playground to play basketball. After dinner during basketball season, he would sit fixated on the TV set watching the Chicago Bulls or his favorite college team, the University of North Carolina Tar Heels (Michael Jordan's alma mater).

Justin dreamed of playing professional basketball like his idol. As he got older, taller, and better at basketball he began looking forward to playing for the varsity team in high school. However, around the time he was to begin his freshman year of high school, he hooked up with a certain pop band, and, well, those plans would have to wait. Since there aren't any independent study basketball teams or correspondence course athletic leagues, Justin had to give up his other dream.

While Justin laments this missed opportunity, he says he holds no regrets. He knew early on that chasing a dream means making sacrifices, and making that dream a reality makes it all worthwhile. "We were sacrificing our lives to do this, and that's something you have to come to grips with," Justin told *Teen Beat*. "If you want this to be your life, you're going to have to give up your other life."

Justin hasn't had to give up on his love of basketball altogether. He still plays whenever he gets the chance, often with his band mates and sometimes even in videos. The lucky guy even got a chance to play hoops with some NBA stars at the MTV Rock 'N Jock game. Justin lived up to his hype, holding his own against the pros, and showing up most of his band mates and the other pop stars who played. However, he did have one not so glamorous moment when six-foot-eleven NBA phenom Kevin Garnett dunked over his head.

"That's not embarrassing to me," Justin told *All-Stars* magazine. "He gets paid 125 million to do that. Like, if [MTV veejay] Carson Daly would have dunked on my head or Tsinina from MTV's *Grind* workout, then I would have been embarrassed. But not Kevin Garnett because that's what he does and I come up to his waist! I can't say I was embarrassed. I was actually like, 'Wow, that's cool!'"

He also collects basketball gear from his favorite teams and players. When he has time, Justin still watches basketball games on TV, only since moving to Orlando, he now roots for Penny Hardaway and the Orlando Magic. But, of course, in his eyes, nobody can touch Michael Jordan.

Big Curly Style

"I think I can speak for all of us when I say we're pretty diverse as a group," Justin explained to *16* magazine. "I think we can go from being very athletic to very dressed up. Some of us are a little more hip-hop and some of us are little more dressy. I think we can go from totally being in warm-up suits to being in suits." Whether he's sportin' cargo pants or decked out in a snazzy white suit like in the "God Must Have Spent a Little More Time on You" video, Justin always looks like a movie star.

Justin loves to go shopping for clothes, and he has an impressive collection of sneakers. He tends to wear baggy jeans, striped sweats, or cargo pants with anything from sports jerseys and T-shirts to sweaters and button shirts. He knows how to be dapper too though. For awards shows, Justin goes all out and wears dark European-cut suits with wide-collared poplin shirts. He especially loves to wear baby blue, his favorite color. Justin knows how to accessorize too. He wears gold hoop earings in both ears, a gold 'N Sync necklace, and he seems to have an endless supply of sunglasses.

Justin's hair is a sensitive subject. "It's the feature that people notice the most about me, I guess," he explained in *Tiger Beat*. "I can't get rid of it, so I have to like it." Until recently, he had trouble taming his tresses, but the stylists who work with 'N Sync have helped him out in that area. Now, Justin keeps it short and uses hair gel to keep it in check. "It's naturally curly," he explained to *Teen Beat* magazine. "The color? The roots are naturally dark. I had this done [the top], but the bottom part is my natural color. It's not that drastic. I'll probably stick with this for a while. I'm thinking of cutting it just a little shorter because it's starting to get a little poofy up here."

8
vital stats & fab facts

Just the Facts

Full Name: Justin Randall Timberlake
Nicknames: Curly, Bounce, Shot, The Baby
Birth Date: January 31, 1981
Zodiac Sign: Aquarius
Birth Place: Memphis, Tennessee
Height: Six feet
Weight: 165 pounds
Eye Color: Blue
Hair Color: Blond
Current Residence: Orlando, Florida
Parents: Lynn and Paul Harless/Randy and Lisa Timberlake

Siblings: Two half brothers, Jonathan, five, and Steven, eight months

Pets: Dog, Ozzie and Cat, Alley

- In addition to performing and playing basketball, Justin stays fit by doing two hundred push-ups every day.
- He also keeps in shape by drinking milk, his favorite drink.
- Justin prefers tea over coffee or cocoa.
- His favorite food is pasta.
- He loves cereal, especially Oreo O's.
- Justin also loves ice cream. His favorite flavor is Daiquiri Ice by Baskin Robbins.
- His favorite word is "crunk"—it means crazy.
- Justin admits to being afraid of snakes.
- Christmas is Justin's favorite holiday.
- One of his favorite things about Christmas is his grandmother's homemade peach cobbler.
- His favorite sport is basketball.
- He roots for the Orlando Magic and the University of North Carolina Tar Heels.

- Michael Jordan, Justin's favorite pro athlete, won a championship at UNC when he was a freshman.
- Justin's favorite color is baby blue, UNC's team color.
- Justin collects basketball gear, sneakers, and candles.
- He also has an impressive collection of sunglasses.
- Justin also likes shopping, working out, and going to the movies.
- Some of his favorite movies include *Twelve Monkeys*, *The Usual Suspects*, and *Ferris Bueller's Day Off*.
- His favorite actors are Brad Pitt and Samuel L. Jackson.
- Meg Ryan and Sandra Bullock are his favorite actresses.
- On the small screen, Justin prefers episodes of *Friends*, *South Park*, *Dawson's Creek*, and *Seinfeld*.
- His favorite book is *Clue*.
- Justin loves to listen to music, especially R&B and hip-hop.

- Justin plays a bit of piano and guitar.
- As a child his favorite toy was a plastic guitar.
- Justin's gone bungee jumping.
- He also hopes to try skydiving someday.
- His greatest fear is to "die unloved."
- In school, Justin's favorite subject was science.
- Math was his least favorite.
- Justin had two cats and two dogs as a kid. One of each is still alive. He says between the two kinds of animals, he prefers dogs.
- On the road, Justin and his band mates usually travel by bus. They only fly if they are traveling more than eight hundred miles.
- Justin once lost his luggage.
- The 'N Sync tour bus features bunk beds, a kitchen, bathroom, stereo, VCR, and gaming system.
- Justin packs along his favorite CDs, videos, and candy for the ride.
- He prefers candy over chocolate and his favorites are Sprees and Runts.
- Justin catches up on rest by taking naps—on buses, airplanes, in airports, anywhere.

- However, he says the slightest sound wakes him.
- He also admits to talking in his sleep.
- He says his most disgusting habit is burping.
- Justin has had several mishaps onstage, including falling and breaking his thumb, and having his pants fall down.
- If he could travel through time, he told *Teen Beat* magazine he'd visit medieval times so he could be a knight.
- Justin carries a chain wallet.
- He also has a cell phone.
- Justin drives a red M-Class Mercedes.
- He also wants to get a sports car.
- Justin loves jewelry, especially gold and diamonds.
- He has a gold necklace that reads, "'N Sync."
- Though he has both ears pierced, Justin has ruled out a nose ring.
- Justin has a flame tattoo. He and his band mates got them together when their debut album went platinum. JC was the only guy to refrain from getting one.

- He considers his personal style to be "athletic hip-hop."
- Justin loves going to the beach . . .
- . . . and to the mountains for some skiing in winter.
- Justin sets his alarm clock to radio. He once woke up to "Tearin' Up My Heart."
- He's received teddy bears, cologne, clothing, and basketballs as gifts from fans.
- Boxers or briefs? Both. Justin opts for boxer-briefs.
- If Justin could change one thing about himself it would be to not procrastinate.
- He wears a size twelve or thirteen shoe ("depending on the shoe").
- Justin's favorite ride at Disney World is Space Mountain.
- Justin recalls crying as a kid when he sat on Santa's lap at a mall.
- When 'N Sync performed on the Miss Teen USA pageant, winner Vanessa Minnillo was enamored of Justin. "I just stared at him the whole time," she said.

9
Justin's jam pack

Though he's a lead singer in a pop band, Justin's personal taste in music is a little different. He says that his biggest musical influence is Stevie Wonder. Meanwhile, in his free time, Justin listens to a variety of sounds, including hip-hop, R&B, and even a little country. (Don't forget, he's from Memphis, Tennessee.)

Justin's CD collection includes the R&B harmonies of Boyz II Men and Take 6, the soulful songs of Brian McKnight, the hip-hop sound of Missy Elliott, and, of course some classic old school by Stevie Wonder. To get a taste of Justin's taste in music, check out some music by these artists.

Stevie Wonder

Supermultitalented Stevie Wonder has an appropriate last name. The singer/songwriter/musician was raised on music, playing harmonica, piano, and drums all by age seven, and he's been blind since birth. In the four decades since, Wonder has put together one of the most marvelous and storied careers in music history. His inspirational rise to the top began with a Motown records recording contract at the age of ten and has culminated with his induction into the Rock and Roll Hall of Fame.

Stevie Wonder's ballads, pop love songs, and soul funk hits have found a place on twenty-nine different solo albums, many of which have gone platinum. Famous singles such as "My Cherie Amour," "Signed, Sealed, Delivered, I'm Yours," "Superstition," "You Are the Sunshine of My Life," "I Just Called to Say I Love You," and "Part-time Lover" have earned Wonder a mind-blowing thirty-six top-ten hits and seventeen Grammy Awards. He's also collaborated on several number one hits, including "Ebony and Ivory," "We Are the World," and "That's What Friends Are For." Indeed, admirer Justin has some awfully big shoes to fill.

Brian McKnight

R&B crooner Brian McKnight is a singer/songwriter/producer/musician and sometime actor. (You may recognize him from guest appearances on *Martin* and *Sister Sister*.) Of course, he is most renowned for his priceless pipes, which have produced four gold records (*Brian McKnight, I Remember You, Anytime,* and *Bethlehem*). Some of Brian's hit songs include "Anytime," which earned him a Best Male Artist nomination at the 1998 MTV Video Music Awards; "You Should Be Mine (Don't Waste Your Time)" featuring Mase, which crossed over and cracked the top ten on both the R&B and pop charts; and "Father," which can be heard on the *Prince Of Egypt* sound-track.

Take 6

Before Boyz II Men, All-4-One, and all the harmony groups that have followed, there was Take 6. Since their debut in 1988, the sextet have awed critics with their beautiful a cappel-la ballads. Their six gold albums have pro-duced a string of hits (such as "I L-O-V-E U" and "All I Need [Is a Chance]"), as well as an astonishing seven Grammy Awards. To get an idea of why Justin and thousands of others have fallen in love with the sounds of Take 6, check out the CDs *So Much 2 Say* and *Join the Band*.

Boyz II Men

The smooth sounding Philadelphia quartet are the top-selling artists in Motown records histo-ry. Their five CDs (*Cooleyhighharmony, Christ-mas Interpretations, II, The Remix Album,* and

Evolution), all multiplatinum, have sold nearly forty million copies, and they are the proud owners of three of the biggest hits in music history—"End of the Road" (number one for thirteen weeks), "I'll Make Love To You" (fourteen weeks), and their collaboration with Mariah Carey, "One Sweet Day" (sixteen weeks). When "I'll Make Love To You" was knocked off from the top slot on the *Billboard* charts, it was replaced by "On Bended Knee," also by Boyz II Men. They are only the third act in history to succeed themselves with a number one hit. The Beatles and Elvis Presley are the others—that's pretty good company.

Missy Elliott

When Missy "Misdemeanor" Elliot isn't creating another hit song mixed with rapping and singing, you can bet she's off collaborating with another artist. For this reason, the talented singer/rapper/songwriter/producer has been dubbed the "Puff Mommy" of hip-hop. Missy's platinum debut album *Supa Dupa Fly* includes three radio hits, "Beep Me 911," "Sock It 2 Me," and "The Rain (Supa Dupa Fly)." In addition to *Supa Dupa Fly*, Missy's talents have been featured on two successful soundtracks, *Woo* and *Why Do Fools Fall In Love*. Missy has produced and recorded singles with some of the most talented artists around, like Aaliyah, Ginuwine, 702, Total, and Melanie "Scary Spice" Brown.

10
number one son

At eighteen, Justin may be the youngest member of 'N Sync, but he's also the oldest, in a sense. Justin is the eldest brother, with two younger siblings, half brothers Jonathan, five, and Steven, eight months. As the first of Lisa Harless and Randy Timberlake's children, Justin is subject to the psychological profile of a firstborn child.

Many psychologists believe there is some significance to birth order. That is, the order in which a person is born in their family (first, middle, or last) can be a determining factor of their personality. Firstborn children generally identify closely with their parents, emulating them as kids and maintaining close ties with them as they mature and grow older.

This is certainly the case with Justin, who puts his family before anything and considers his mom one of his best friends. Of all the members of 'N Sync, Justin is the most likely to get homesick, and for this reason, he carries a cell phone and calls home every day. In the *Home for Christmas* liner notes, Justin thanked his family for "their undying love and support."

Justin's birth father, Randy, who was in a bluegrass band, was a strong influence on Justin's musical aspirations. Similarly, Justin's mom, Lynn, encouraged his passion for music at every turn. Whether it was singing to him, playing music for him, or driving him to choir and later auditions, Lynn was always helping Justin follow his dream.

Big Bro

While there's no need for Justin to keep his older and equally enthusiastic band mates in line, he does play big brother with his little bros at home. He baby-sits, plays with them, and even spoils them rotten. Every year, Justin buys five-year-old Jonathan a new pair of Nike Air Jordan sneakers for his birthday. "Anything I'm into, he's into," Justin told *Tiger Beat* magazine.

Imitation is the sincerest form of flattery, right, Justin? "Yeah, yeah. He watches us on TV, so he mimics us," he told *Teen Beat* magazine. "For his birthday, my dad ordered him a miniature stage with a cordless microphone and a one-monitor sound system. He gets up there and does our whole show! He knows all the words to our songs. It's just hilarious." Move over, Aaron Carter!

Justin has an equal, if not more adorable, sweet spot for his littlest sib. Jonathan may sing like Justin, but baby Steven, who was born on August 14, 1998, looks like him. "When he was born I got word from my Daddy that he looked exactly like my one-month-old pictures," he told *16* magazine. With looks and talent, some day in the future little Jonathan and baby Steven may need some career advice from their famous big brother.

Solid As a Rock

Firstborn children are typically responsible. Justin is no exception. As much as Justin loves a good time or a good laugh, he's a pillar of responsibility when it comes to his music career. Being a part of a world-famous pop group means following a difficult schedule and putting in long hours. Justin is always up to the task. "He's got a really good head on his shoulders," Chris told *Tiger Beat* magazine. "When it's time to work, he's always there."

Justin recognizes that he's had to make many sacrifices to be a part of 'N Sync. But he realizes that being away from home, and giving up school, friends, and basketball is just the price he must pay to fulfill his dream. Justin gets up early when he wants to sleep and stays in and rests many nights when he wants to go out. On sunny days, when he'd like to be playing ball, he's in rehearsals or in the studio. It's all worth it to Justin, who wouldn't give up traveling the world and performing for fans for anything, except maybe his family.

11
something fishy

Justin is an Aquarius born January 31. Based on astrology, Aquarius, the sign of those born between January 20 and February 19, is considered to be the most richly endowed and highly developed of the twelve zodiac signs. People born under this sign are said to have an overwhelming number of positive attributes, so many that Aquarians are considered to be inspirational. A high proportion of world leaders, celebrities, and professional athletes were born under this sign. As a famous, multitalented singer/dancer and athlete, Justin is a model Aquarian.

He'll Go Down in History

Typical to his sign, Justin gets along well with others, but is very much an individual. Though this independent mindedness can sometimes lead to bouts of rebellion (which Justin has admitted to in his younger years), it also makes an Aquarian a strong leader. Many born under this sign possess an imagination and inventiveness that goes far beyond the normal realm of creativity. Aquarians are versatile, being equally adept in both arts and sciences. Coupled with a penchant for high aspirations, it's no surprise that countless Aquarians have gone on to not only lead by example, but to make history.

Some Aquarian leaders include Presidents Abraham Lincoln, Franklin D. Roosevelt, and Ronald Reagan; Generals Douglas MacArthur and Omar Bradley; labor movement leader Samuel Gompers; and aviator Charles Lindbergh. Dozens of brilliant writers like Charles Dickens, Lewis Carroll, James Joyce, Sinclair

Lewis, Gertrude Stein, Norman Mailer, and James Michener are Aquarians. Other notable Aquarians include singer Leontyne Price; comedian Jack Benny; actors John Barrymore, Clark Gable, and Mia Farrow; and baseball legend Jackie Robinson. Indeed, being an Aquarian puts Justin in with some select company!

It's All Good

Aquarians are also fascinated by many different things and have quite an affinity for learning. Eleventh-sign folks are often the first to grasp a new concept and are never afraid to try new things like languages and instruments. Aquarians also typically have excellent memories. Because of their vast knowledge and ability to lead, Aquarians often follow a career path in teaching or politics. Their many talents and open mind make them prime candidates to become entertainers or writers.

On the social front, Aquarians can get along with virtually any type of person. The Aquarian is open, friendly, and approachable without bias. They have a boundless liking for humanity and are quick to make new friends, though typically an Aquarian already has more than he/she can count. In astrology the Aquarian is often referred to as "everyone's friend." The only type of person the Aquarian shuns is one who is narrow minded, particularly if the person is prejudiced.

Before you begin to think that Aquarians are perfect, here are a few not so admirable traits common to people born under the eleventh sign. Aquarians are commonly impatient and may get frustrated waiting in line, or being stuck in traffic. Aquarians are often procrastinators (Justin says this is the one thing he'd change about himself), but their tardiness never seems to bother anyone because their apologies are so endearing. Aquarians tend to exaggerate, and are also often suckers for flattery.

Lucky in Love

On the romance front, Aquarians are tender-hearted and often lucky in love. The Aquarian male never lacks female admirers. We don't need to see Justin's birth certificate, thank you—he's an Aquarius. Aquarians are interested in far more than just outward appearances. They commonly seek a partner who is their friend above all else. A warm person with similar traits and interests who is a good conversationalist makes a good match.

The male Aquarian desires affection but can't stand to be smothered. This fine line must be adhered to for a relationship to work, because Aquarians need their freedom. Don't forget how much they like their friends. Aquarians demand honesty in a relationship. Guys born under the eleventh sign take relationships seriously and devote considerable energy to making love last and their girl happy. Aquarians can be a lot of fun to date, too.

They are typically spontaneous, considerate, and affectionate. And though it may be a bit premature to consider this, Aquarian males also make great fathers.

12
here comes the rooster

One of the sacrifices that any pop star has to make is giving up sleeping in. Just like folks in the military, professional musicians often have to get up at the crack of dawn. Whether it's for a video shoot, rehearsal, or to catch an early overseas flight, the snooze button simply isn't an option. Justin has adapted to this rise-and-shine lifestyle like a crowing rooster.

While he doesn't actually ever scream cock-a-doodle-doo at 5 A.M. (Chris probably wouldn't care for this), Justin is a rooster, in one sense. In Chinese astrology, Justin was born (1981) in the year of the Rooster. This ancient study, which dates back at least 350 years to the Ming Dynasty, uses time of birth to assess a person's potential and what the future holds for them. Each birth year in the Chinese Zodiac is named for a particular animal—Rooster, Rat, Ox, Tiger, Rabbit, Dragon, Snake, Horse, Goat, Monkey, Dog, or Pig. The theory is that people born in a particular year take on some of the characteristics of that animal.

Rooster Boy

Rooster people are not difficult nuts to crack. They are typically honest, straightforward, and tell it exactly like it is. Like the animal, those born under this sign are extremely observant, almost to the point of having a sixth sense. Roosters have cautious, skeptical minds, and for this reason, it is difficult to fool them.

Roosters are multitalented, sharp-minded, and enthusiastic, a powerful combination that makes career opportunities almost endless. Creative careers in fields such as music are a good possibility, especially when you consider that three of the most famous composers in history, Wagner, Verdi, and Rachmaninoff, were all Roosters.

Roosters are also practical and resourceful. However, they also like to dream. This makes relationships difficult because reality often doesn't live up to a dream, but the Rooster never stops looking for the perfect match. Typically, the Rooster is compatible with the Snake, Ox, and Pig. Goats and other Roosters make terrible matches.

The Rooster is fiercely loyal and makes a devoted friend. They keep promises and secrets and are always reliable. They'll stop short of nothing to make a loved one smile. The Rooster loves to entertain guests and doesn't mind being the center of attention. In fact, Roosters are suckers for flattery and dress flashily to encourage it. Roosters are often vain, but then, they are so distinctively attractive they can't help but draw attention to themselves.

So, what does the future hold for the Rooster? 1999 is the year of the Rabbit. According to Chinese astrology, this should be a good year for Roosters, with lots of positive change. Though the changes can become unsettling, they are all for the better. The Rabbit year should bring continued success, as well as changes in career, social life, and family dynamic for the Rooster. Stay tuned.

13
just the one for Justin

When you're a world-traveling pop star with throngs of girls chasing after you at every stop, you can afford to be choosy when it comes to dating. Though Justin is single now, he makes little attempt to hide his interest in girls. But since Justin doesn't have time for school right now and he's too young to go with some of his band mates to dance clubs, how could he possibly meet a nice, single young girl? There are several thousand at every 'N Sync concert begging to be asked on a date by the guy some on-line fans in a chat room referred to as kitten boy. Why? "Because he's cuddly, playful, mischievous, and so cute you want to scream!"

If he's all that he must have his sights set

really high, right? He probably only wants to date an actress or a model, right? Come on, give the sweet Memphis guy some credit. Justin isn't the shallow type. He's not looking for a living Barbie doll or a celebrity name, just a little companionship. He does have somewhat of a discerning eye, but it's not about looks where Justin's concerned. Keep reading to see who's right for Mister Right.

Crushed with Eyeliner

Though he's never been in love, Justin told *16* magazine, "I've been infatuated and had a few crushes." Justin's very first crush was on his uncle's girlfriend who he recalls "was very pretty." Justin went on to find people his own age, and had his first date and kiss in sixth grade. A year later he had his first girlfriend, a girl named Mindy, who he met at Disney World through *The Mickey Mouse Club.*

As an adolescent, Justin admits to have had a crush on fellow pop star Janet Jackson. He even had her poster up on his bedroom wall. Who'd have thought he'd end up opening up for her concert tour with his world-famous group just a few years later! In an interview with *Teen Beat* magazine Justin kidded, "I'm a big fan of Janet Jackson. She doesn't know that she's gonna marry me."

Since becoming a pop star in his own right, Justin's admitted to having a crush on dance-pop star Robyn. Justin got to meet her when 'N Sync was recording their debut CD in Stockholm, Sweden. "I left my heart in Sweden," he told *16* magazine. "Robyn's from Sweden and she's the cutest thing and she's friendly, so you've got to move there."

I Want That One

Justin says his ideal girl would be "confident, humble, sensitive, and with a good sense of humor." On a first date with a girl, Justin says he'd try to "sweep her off her feet." He may mean that literally, because he's also said he likes a spontaneous and adventurous girl who isn't afraid to, say, try bungee jumping.

If Justin were to meet such a girl, where would he take her on a date? "My idea of a perfect date is just hanging at home, having a video night. A good conversation is the biggest turn-on. I'm looking for a girl with confidence. There's nothing sexier," he revealed in *YM* magazine.

In an America Online interview, JC said, "Justin's a real charmer; the ladies love him." But again, Justin can't date them all, so who's it gonna be? "Somebody who I can have fun with because I always like to go out and have fun," Justin added. "And somebody who will listen to what I have to say because I talk too much."

In Q&A session with *All-Stars* magazine, Justin talked about the importance of having a good outlook on life. "It's hard to find a girl who's positive about anything these days," he offered. "Optimism—that's what I'm looking for! A little optimism in a world of sarcasm and pessimism.'' That's a lot of isms. Is making a commitment when Justin finally does find just the right girl a certainty? ''I'm not waiting for it to happen, but I won't run away from it when it does,'' Justin told *Tiger Beat* magazine.

14
'n the future

After their first full year on the American pop scene produced two platinum albums, three hit songs, a sold-out tour, and enough fans to populate a city, what will 'N Sync do for an encore? Keep on truckin'! Through the middle of May 1999, they'll continue selling out concert arenas all over the U.S. After that, they'll take a short break to promote their next album and then begin a world tour.

As of January 1999, 'N Sync had written some songs and were hoping to squeeze in some time in the studio for recording. One thing that likely will change is that Justin and his co—lead singer, JC, will look to build on their first foray into songwriting in *Home for Christmas.* Justin will no doubt have more of a hand in the creative process behind the next 'N Sync album, be it writing, producing, instrumentation, or just song selection.

By the time their U.S. tour is over, they hope to have enough songs written, and that their record company can hook them up with some great producers, for studio work this spring. A new 'N Sync album should be expected by the summer of 1999. Meanwhile, here's where you can find them on tour.

March

3	Jacksonville, FL	Jacksonville Coliseum
5	Greenville, NC	Bi-Lo Center
6	Chapel Hill, NC	Dean Smith Center
7	Charleston, SC	WV Coliseum
8	Pittsburgh, PA	Civic Center
9	Albany, NY	Pepsi Arena
11	Providence, RI	Civic Center
12	Hempstead, NY	Nassau Coliseum
13	New Haven, CT	Coliseum
16	Boston, MA	Fleet Center
18	Philadelphia, PA	First Union Center

19	Washington, DC	MCI Center
20	Hampton, VA	Coliseum
21	Charlotte, NC	Coliseum
23	Columbus, OH	Schottenstein
24	Auburn Hills, MI	Palace
25	Cleveland, OH	Gund Arena
27	Chicago, IL	Rosemont Horizon
28	Grand Rapids, MI	Van Andel Arena
30	Nashville, TN	Arena

April

1	Kansas City, MO	Kemper Arena
2	St. Louis, MO	Kiel Center
3	Cincinnati, OH	Crown Arena
6	Lafayette, LA	Cajun Dome
7	Houston, TX	Compaq Center
8	Dallas, TX	Reunion Arena
9	Oklahoma City, OK	Myriad
10	Wichita, KS	Coliseum
13	Phoenix, AZ	America West Center
15	San Diego, CA	Cox or Sports Arena
16	Los Angeles, CA	Great Western Forum
17	Las Vegas, NV	MGM Grand or Mandalay Bay

18	Anaheim, CA	The Pond
19	Oakland, CA	Coliseum
22	Portland, OR	Rose Quarter
23	Tacoma, WA	Tacoma Dome
25	Spokane, WA	Arena
27	Boise, ID	Idaho Center
28	Salt Lake City, UT	E Center or Delta Center

May
12	Tampa, FL	Ice Palace
13	Orlando, FL	Orlando Arena
16	Ft. Lauderdale, FL	National Car Center

Note: Dates subject to change. Additional shows may be added.

Justin's Crystal Ball

Outside of the band, Justin's future plans involve finding more time for his family, finding himself a girlfriend, and, eventually, going to college. Though in order to join 'N Sync, he was willing to postpone his college plans and complete his high school curriculum through independent study, Justin never had any intention of abandoning them all together. Throughout school Justin was a straight-A student who was particularly adept at math and science. When he was on *The Mickey Mouse Club*, Justin said that a performing-arts degree would help him further his career as a singer, comedian, or actor. In the long run, whatever road Justin travels, be it in entertainment or not, success and fulfillment are certain to follow.

Does Justin have any goals for the near future? Sure. In a *BB* magazine feature, Justin talked about his 1999 New Year's resolution, to devote more of his free time to resting. During the European leg of 'N Sync's tour, Justin said, "I was getting maybe two or three hours of sleep a night. I'd wake up and still be in a daze. I'd be a zombie or something." What does he plan to do about it? "I'm going to get more rest. I think that's a good resolution."

In the distant future, the sky's the limit for the megatalented, supergorgeous Justin. With his determination and work ethic, he could probably do just about anything he put his mind to—learn new instruments, produce, act, or even go solo. However, for now at least, Justin is perfectly content to succeed as a part of 'N Sync. "I don't think that's in any of our heads at this particular moment in time," Justin told *Smash Hits* magazine. "We're just focusing on 'N Sync at this time. We just want this to be the best that it can possibly be, and that's why we're devoting all of our time and attention to this."

u'NSYNCable

Despite 'N Sync's startling success, when Justin looks at the group, he still sees room for improvement. "When we see ourselves on TV, we start critiquing from the minute we see it, and we want to keep taking steps forward," he told *Teen Beat* magazine. Justin says the keys to success are "determination and practice."

Without question, 'N Sync's performances will get better with each concert, and their current tour should give them plenty of practice.

Another thing that will make 'N Sync's concerts even better is the influx of greater finances and more resources at their disposal. The bigger the band, the bigger the production, as Justin explained in *Billboard* magazine. "The more success, the bigger the toys are to play with, so now it's getting really fun. Now we can use props and think more creatively. Our boundaries are becoming bigger and bigger, and we can fantasize and come up with things on a bigger scale."

"It's going to get a little bigger," Justin told *Teen Beat* magazine. "We're just stepping up, moving to the next level." How much better can these guys get?

In order to approach the greatness of some of Justin's idols, like Stevie Wonder and Boyz II Men, 'N Sync needs to prove themselves over the long haul. As they gain more experience, exposure, and confidence, longevity will follow. But while Justin and his band

mates may aspire to someday be legendary
like his idols, he pointed out to *16* magazine
that "I don't think that 'N Sync wants to
emulate anybody. We want to be pioneers in
the music industry. We want to make our own
name."

15
keep in touch

If you're looking for more information about Justin and 'N Sync, or just ways to contact them, you've come to the right place. Following is a resource guide to give you direction in your 'N Sync quest. Whether you're trying to find an address where to send a Valentine's Day card for Justin, or some superdetailed information like what kind of shampoo he uses, this handy-dandy reference section should help you out.

You've Got Mail

There are many ways you can contact Justin, JC, Lance, Chris, and Joey. You can send letters, cards, drawings, poems, or whatever to

'N Sync's record company, agency, or management offices. You may get a response or a photo in return, but don't count on it. With 'N Sync's worldwide popularity, thousands of pieces of mail arrive at those addresses daily. If you're really determined, then put on your thinking cap and do something supercreative to make your parcel stand out from the rest. Think artistic, different, big, bold, bright, and colorful. Give your letter a personal touch, by including stickers or drawings of some of Justin's favorite things on the outside of the envelope.

If you're going to send Justin a gift, give a lot of thought to what you send. You don't have to spend any money (poems, drawings, recipes). Want to know what Justin likes best? "Ya know what's cool? When they send us videos dancing to our music or mimicking us, acting like us," he told *Teen Machine* magazine.

If you want to receive correspondence from 'N Sync, then your best bet is to join the fan club. For a small fee, you'll receive a membership pack that includes either photos, stickers, or posters, followed by newsletter updates. If you're one of those fanatics whose bedroom wall is completely covered with Justin pinups, and whose closet is brimming with 'N Sync T-shirts, hats, and sweatshirts, then you'll want to call for a merchandise catalog.

Official Fan Club: 'N Sync Fan Club
PO Box 692109
Orlando, FL 32869-2109

Fan Club 'N Sync
PO Box 0617
D-94307 Straubing,
  Germany

Record Company: c/o RCA Records
1540 Broadway
New York, NY 10036

c/o RCA Records
6363 Sunset Blvd.
Hollywood, CA 90028

c/o BMG Music Canada
150 John St.
Toronto, Ontario
   M5V 3C3 Canada

c/o BMG/RCA Records
Hedford House
#9-78 Folham High St.
London, SW5 3JW, UK

c/o BMG Ariola
Carl Bertelsmann-Stasse
   270
D-33311, Gütersloh,
   Germany

Management: c/o Trans Continental
    Entertainment
7380 Sand Lake Rd.
Suite 350
Orlando, FL 32189

Talent Agency: c/o Renaissance
                        Entertainment
                        1501 Broadway
                        Suite 1301
                        New York, NY 10036

Merchandise: 1-415-575-6644

Hot Off the Stove

If you can't seem to get enough juicy information about Justin and 'N Sync, then hop on-line. Whether you're looking for the up-to-the-minute info, gossip, or a chance to make friends with other 'N Sync fans, the Internet is the place to be. Check out 'N Sync's official websites (www.nsync.com) for the latest news, tour dates, and TV appearances, bio data, band e-mail, fan club and merchandise info, plus a multimedia link to music and videos.

Also keep an eye out for 'N Sync live chats on America Online and at Yahoo.com (two are scheduled for March, 1999). In one AOL chat,

Justin said, "Check out our web page—we think it's awesome. We're usually hangin' out there, chatting, so you can usually find us there."

Via Internet:
Official Websites   http://www.nsync.com

BMG/RCA Records   http://www.bmg.com/
                                       rca/artists/nsync
                                       http://www.bmg-
                                       backstage.com

You can find more 'N Sync info and more 'N Sync fans at the record company websites as well as at the more than two thousand fan-produced sites. That's right, that's no misprint. Just plug in the two words "Justin Timberlake" into the Dogpile search. If you're not familiar with Dogpile (www.dogpile.com), it's a composite World Wide Web search that uses all of the most popular search engines, like Yahoo!, InfoSeek, Excite, Lycos, GoTo.com,

Thunderstone, WebCrawler, Magellan, What U Seek, and AltaVista. At the time this book was written, nearly twenty-five hundred matches came up for "Justin Timberlake." Granted some of them were repeat mentions, and others were probably incorrect matches, but nonetheless, that's an astounding number.

You can use any of those search engines to find websites devoted to 'N Sync and/or Justin Timberlake. Narrow your search (entertainment/music/artists/) to save time and avoid confusion. If you use America Online, you can also try keyword: ' N Sync. Many of the fan-produced websites are merely single pages that pay homage to the producer's crush—for instance, a single picture of Justin with a caption that reads, "Justin Timberlake is the hottest guy in the whole wide world!" Still other sites are poorly produced and contain technical glitches that will either make your monitor freeze or your computer crash.

However, if you've got the time and the patience, there are some really cool 'N Sync websites out there that fans went to a lot

of trouble to create. Many feature hard-
to-find photos from around the world and e-
mail addresses so you can swap photos and
info with other 'N Sync fanatics. There are
also links to other pages, chat rooms, and
loads and loads of rumors. Chat rooms are a
great way to meet fellow fans, but remember,
don't believe everything you read. Here are
a few suggestions. Good luck and happy
hunting.

www.nsyncworld.com
http://www.peeps.com
www.angelfire.com/nj/justinsfanpage/
   index.html
www.angelfire.com/hi/justintimberlake/
   index.html
www.gurlpages.com/music/justintgirl/
   index.html
www.starbuzz.com/guide/J/
   Justin_Timberlake.html
www.geocities.com/hollywood/cinema/2851
www.geocities.com/paris/cafe/7063
www.geocities.com/paris/lights/6875

www.geocities.com/sunsetstrip/towers/6354
www.geocities.com/sunsetstrip/stage/5955
www.geocities.com/sunsetstrip/backstage/
  8442
www.geocities.com/timessquare/stadium/3713
www.geocities.com/timessquare/stadium/1347

16
trivia time

1. Where was Justin Timberlake born?
2. What is his birthday?
3. What's his zodiac sign?
4. What is Justin's middle name?

5. What is his mom's name?
6. What is his stepfather's name?
7. How many siblings does Justin have?
8. What are their names?
9. Justin has a dog named:
   a) Harriet b) Ozzie c) Dizzy d) Rudolph
10. Justin's favorite sport is:
    a) basketball b) golf c) baseball d) soccer
11. What is Justin's favorite 'N Sync song?
12. Which of the following nicknames does Justin goes by? (Choose as many as apply.)
    a) J.R. b) Bounce c) Air Timberlake d) Curly
13. True or False: Justin sleepwalks.
14. Justin's favorite word is:
    a) phat b) dope c) crunk d) slammin'
15. What animal is Justin afraid of?
16. True or False: Justin's favorite pro athlete is Shaquille O'Neal.
17. What is Justin's favorite color?
18. Which of the following things doesn't Justin collect?
    a) candles b) sneakers c) Beanie Babies d) sports jerseys

19. Justin's CD collection includes discs by all of the following artists except one.
a) Big Bad Voodoo Daddy b) Brian Mc-Knight c) Missy Elliot d) Stevie Wonder

20. True or False: Justin sang in the church choir as a boy.

21. Who thought up the name 'N Sync?

22. What other member of 'N Sync was on *The Mickey Mouse Club* with Justin?

23. For how many years was Justin on the *MMC* show?

24. Which of the following celebrities is not an *MMC* alumnus?
a) Keri Russell b) Britney Spears c) Christina Aguilera d) Katie Holmes

25. What sport does Justin play in the "I Want You Back" video?

26. In the "Tearin' Up My Heart" video Justin sings to the camera while lying on: a) a couch b) a bed c) a recliner d) the floor

27. During the filming of "For the Girl Who Has Everything," Justin and what other

member of 'N Sync got toppled by a wave?

28. What color outfits do the 'N Sync guys all wear throughout the entire "God Must Have Spent a Little More Time on You" video?

29. What former child star makes a cameo appearance in the "Merry Christmas, Happy Holidays" video?

30. In what 'N Sync song does Justin sing the following lyric: "I never thought that love could feel like this, when you changed my world with just one kiss"?

31. Justin has a poster hanging in his room of what famous female pop singer?

32. True or False: Justin often wears a gold necklace that says " 'N Sync."

33. Justin says his most prized possession is: a) his voice b) his basketball c) a Stevie Wonder autograph d) a pinkie ring

34. What daily exercise does Justin do to stay in shape?

35. True or False: The "I Want You Back" video was filmed in New York City.

36. In what country did Justin fall onstage and break his thumb?
37. Which two members of 'N Sync live with Justin and his mom?
38. Where do they live?
39. What kind of car does Justin drive?
40. Which of the following is one of Justin's favorite foods:
    a) pasta b) mackerel c) liver d) yams
41. What was Justin's favorite childhood toy?
42. What is Justin's favorite TV sitcom?
43. Which of the following is *not* one of his favorite movies:
    a) *Shakespeare In Love* b) *Ferris Bueller's Day Off* c) *12 Monkeys* d) *The Usual Suspects*
44. True or False: Justin's favorite holiday is Halloween.
45. True or False: Justin's mom, Lynn, now manages pop groups.
46. How old was Justin when 'N Sync formed?
47. What other famous musicians were born in Memphis?

48. According to Chinese Astrology, Justin was born in the year of what animal?

49. How many websites are devoted to Justin and 'N Sync:

   a) seven b) about one hundred c) about five hundred d) over two thousand

50. True or False: Justin's gone bungee jumping.

51. Justin's worst habit is:

   a) snoring b) biting his nails c) burping

52. Given a choice between money, love, and fame, Justin chooses . . . ?

53. Which of the following magazine covers *hasn't* 'N Sync appeared on:

   a) *Tiger Beat* b) *Teen People* c) *16* d) *Spin*

54. What is the address for 'N Sync's official website?

55. In which of the following countries has 'N Sync performed:

   a) England b) Australia c) Japan d) all of the above

56. 'N Sync has sold out concert arenas in which of the following cities:

a) Orlando b) Milwaukee c) Dallas d) all of the above

57. During what song does 'N Sync encourage audience participation by yelling, "When I say, 'N' you say, 'Sync' "?

58. What Christmas song did Justin cowrite?

59. True or False: Justin has a girlfriend.

60. When he was ten, Justin was in a group that imitated a pop group. Which of the following groups was it:
a) Color Me Badd b) Kool & The Gang c) New Kids On the Block d) The Jackson 5

61. What does Justin miss most when he's on the road?

62. Who said the following: "He's just got that star quality. When people see Justin on stage, they think he's really cool."?

63. Which other pop act do people (okay, stodgy adults who wouldn't know a Furby from a Flow-bee) often confuse with 'N Sync:
a) Backstreet Boys b) Hanson c) Five d) The Moffatts

64. What two female singers joined 'N Sync on the Disney Channel's *Holidays In Concert* special?

65. Which member of 'N Sync was found through Justin's vocal coach?

Answers to TRIVIA TIME

1. Memphis, Tennessee
2. January 31, 1981
3. Aquarius
4. Randall
5. Lynn Harless
6. Paul Harless
7. Two
8. Jonathan and Steven
9. b
10. a
11. "God Must Have Spent A Little More Time On You"
12. b and d
13. False, he talks in his sleep.
14. c

15. Snakes
16. False, it's Michael Jordan.
17. Baby blue
18. c
19. a
20. True
21. Justin's mom
22. JC Chasez
23. Two
24. d
25. Basketball
26. b
27. Chris Kirkpatrick
28. White
29. Gary Coleman
30. "God Must Have Spent a Little More Time on You"
31. Janet Jackson
32. True
33. a
34. Push-ups.
35. False, it was recorded on a set.
36. Germany

37. JC Chasez and Chris Kirkpatrick
38. Orlando, Florida
39. M-Class Mercedes
40. a
41. A plastic guitar
42. *Seinfeld*
43. a
44. False, it's Christmas
45. True
46. Fourteen
47. Elvis Presley and Jerry Lee Lewis
48. Rooster
49. d
50. True
51. c
52. Love
53. d
54. www.nsync.com
55. d
56. d
57. "Tearin' Up My Heart"
58. "Merry Christmas, Happy Holidays"
59. False!

60. c
61. His family
62. JC Chasez
63. a
64. Shawn Colvin and Tatyana Ali
65. Lance Bass

Scoring

Add up your total number of correct answers and see how much you know about Justin Timberlake and 'N Sync!

56–65 correct: You're a crunk fanatic! Are you sure you're not Justin's next-door neighbor?

36–55 correct: Nice going! You're definitely 'n tune with 'N Sync.

25–35 correct: Not bad. You may know something about Justin, but not enough to be an 'N Sync fanatic.

11–24 correct: You've got some research to do. Better start readin' up on 'N Sync before you embarrass yourself in front of other fans.

0–10 correct: Huh?! You call yourself an 'N Sync fan?

About the Author

Matt Netter is the author of the *New York Times* best-seller *'N Sync: Tearin' Up The Charts*. He's written biographies on many other pop music sensations, including Backstreet Boys, Aaron Carter, Hanson, and Five. Matt's currently in his hometown of New York City scouting out the next great pop group.

DON'T MISS ANY OF OUR
BEST-SELLING POP MUSIC BIOS!

Backstreet Boys ☆ Aaron Carter
by Matt Netter

Five
by Matt Netter

Dancin' With Hanson
by Ravi

Hanson: Mmmbop to the Top
by Jill Matthews

Isaac Hanson: Totally Ike!
by Nancy Krulik

Taylor Hanson: Totally Taylor!
by Nancy Krulik

Zac Hanson: Totally Zac!
by Matt Netter

Hanson: The Ultimate Trivia Book
by Matt Netter

Jewel: Pieces of a Dream
by Kristen Kemp

Pop Quiz
by Nancy Krulik

'N Sync: Tearin' Up the Charts
by Matt Netter

Will Smith: Will Power!
by Jan Berenson

Five

The members of Five, Britain's hot new boy band, met last year at a London talent search and things "just clicked." Since that fateful day, these lovable lads—Rich, Sean, Scott, Abs, and J—have carried out a full-scale British Invasion of the U.S. pop scene with their edgy blend of soul, hip-hop, rap, and some serious attitude, creating a unique sound that blows the competition away.

With the complete 411 on these bright British stars, this book will leave you "Satisfied"!

By Matt Netter

Available now!

POCKET BOOKS

Published by Pocket Books

2087

98° and rising to the top!

The mercury's rising, thanks to 98°, the hottest new band around! Jeff, Justin, and brothers Nick and Drew have won the respect of Motown—and the hearts of thousands of fans—with their unique mix of R&B, pop, Euro-dance, and hip-hop. Get all the answers to your questions about the band that's setting the charts on fire!

By Nancy Krulik

Available in April 1999!